SAFETY FIRST

Safety in the Water

Joanne Mattern
ABDO Publishing Company

visit us at
www.abdopub.com

Published by Abdo Publishing Company 4940 Viking Drive, Edina, Minnesota 55435. Copyright © 1999 by Abdo Consulting Group, Inc. International copyrights reserved in all countries. No part of this book may be reproduced in any form without written permission from the publisher.

Printed in the United States.

Photo credits: Peter Arnold, Inc., Super Stock

Edited by Julie Berg
Contributing editor Morgan Hughes
Graphics by Linda O'Leary

Library of Congress Cataloging-in-Publication Data

Mattern, Joanne, 1963-
    Safety in the water / Joanne Mattern.
    p. cm. -- (Safety first)
    Includes index.
    Summary: Offers some simple safety rules to follow when swimming or boating.
    ISBN 1-57765-072-7
    1. Aquatic sports--Safety measures--Juvenile literature. [1. Aquatic sports--Safety measures. 2. Safety.] I. Title. II. Series.
    GV770.6.M38   1999
    796.2'0028'9--dc21
                                      98-17278
                                            CIP
                                          AC

Contents

Safety First!

There's no better way to keep cool than to go for a swim or take a ride in a boat. Whether you swim in a pool, in a lake, in a river, or in the ocean, getting wet is a great way to have fun!

But playing in the water can also be **dangerous**. You'll have a lot more fun if you practice staying safe. Staying safe means you won't get hurt. You won't get in trouble. And you will keep other people from getting hurt or in trouble, too!

How can you stay safe in the water? The best way is to follow the rules and think before you act. This book will show you many ways to always put safety first while you are swimming or boating.

Swimming is more fun when you play safely.

Swim with a Buddy

You should never swim or play around water by yourself. Bring a friend or family member along any time you go near the water. Even if your **companion** doesn't want to swim, he or she can still help you stay safe. A swimming buddy can help if you get into trouble. If the problem is too big for the two of you to handle, one of you can run for help.

Opposite page: Always swim with a buddy.

Watching Out for You

Friends and swimming buddies are important. But it's even more important to have an adult **supervise** you in the water. The adult might be a **lifeguard** or a parent. It could be a baby-sitter or a relative. No matter who it is, an adult should stay near the water to watch you. That way, there will always be someone able to help if you get into trouble.

Opposite page:
A lifeguard on duty.

Safety by the Pool

If you've ever heard a **lifeguard** yell, "No running by the pool," you've heard an important safety rule. What's so bad about running by the pool? The area around it is usually wet. Your feet are wet, too. All that water makes it easy to slip and fall. If you fall, you could hurt yourself or someone else.

Another reason why it's **dangerous** to run by a pool is the edges are usually made of **concrete**. Concrete is very hard and rough. If you fall, you could hurt yourself badly.

*Opposite page:
Be especially
careful when swimming
in a crowded pool.*

Safe Swimming

Once you get in the water, there are many safety rules to remember. If you aren't a good swimmer, use an inner tube or a **flotation device** to help you stay above water.

If you aren't a good swimmer, stay in the **shallow** water. Even if you can swim, it's best to go into deep water with a friend or an adult. In a pool or on a public beach, a rope usually marks the deep water.

Flotation devices help keep your head above water.

If you are swimming in a river or lake, be careful not to get into water that is too deep for you. You might step from **shallow** water into deep water very quickly. Or you could slip into a hole. Be sure to **wade** and swim carefully until you know where the **dangerous** spots are.

Be careful swimming in the ocean, too. Watch out for strong currents called **undertows**. They can pull you away from shore. Look out for jellyfish. This creature has a nasty sting!

A drop-off is a hidden hazard to watch for.

Diving Safety

Diving is lots of fun. But it can also be very **dangerous**. If you don't know how to dive, ask an adult to teach you.

Never run on a **diving board**. Because it is wet, the board can be slippery. The steps up to the diving board are slippery, too. Climb them slowly and carefully.

If you get onto the diving board and feel scared, don't panic. Turn around or back up slowly until you reach the back of the board. Then you can climb or step down. You can always try again later.

Make sure other swimmers are out of the way before you dive.

You should never dive in **shallow** water. It's easy to hit your head if the water isn't deep enough. Pools and public beaches usually have areas marked for safe diving. Be sure to dive only in these areas.

Only dive in areas specially marked for diving.

Look before You Dive

Another important diving rule is to look before you dive. This is really important if you're swimming in a lake or a river. Before you dive, look to see if there are any rocks, logs, or other objects hidden under the water that could hurt you.

You should also be careful not to dive on top of other swimmers. Before you jump in, make sure no one is swimming underneath you. If someone has

Sharp objects hidden under the water can be dangerous.

dived in ahead of you, give that person time to swim out of the way before you dive into the water. The best way to stay safe is to only dive in areas that are marked. You can also ask the **lifeguard** if an area is safe for diving.

Never dive into unknown water.

Life Jackets

Sailing or riding in a boat is a great way to keep cool on a warm summer day. If it is hot, you might want to just wear your bathing suit or a T-shirt and shorts. But there's one piece of clothing you should always have on: a **life jacket**.

Life jackets float. Some life jackets also have special bands that reflect light, so they are easy to spot in the water. Some life jackets have whistles to use for calling help.

Life jackets can help you stay safe. That is why it is important to always wear one when you are on a boat. In some states, it is the law. Ask your family and friends to wear their life jackets, too.

Don't go boating without a life jacket.

Boating Safety

If you are riding in a small boat or a **canoe**, never stand up or walk around. Small boats, like canoes, can tip easily. Standing or walking around in a boat can rock it enough that it will tip over, or **capsize**.

There are many other safety rules to follow on a boat. If your family has a boat, it's a good idea to take a boat safety course. A course will help you learn many important rules. And the more you know, the easier it is to always put safety first!

Opposite page:
Learn safety rules
before you ride in
a canoe.

Glossary

Canoe (kah-NOO) - a narrow boat that you move through the water by paddling.

Capsize (KAP-size) - to turn over in the water.

Companion (kuhm-PAN-yuhn) - someone with whom you spend time.

Concrete (KON-kreet) - a building material made from sand, gravel, cement, and water.

Dangerous (DAYN-jur-uhss) - likely to cause harm; not safe.

Diving board (DYE-ving bord) - a long wooden or plastic board that sticks out over the deep end of a swimming pool.

Flotation device (floh-TAY-shun di-VISE) - a plastic or foam object that allows a person to float in water.

Lifeguard (LIFE-gard) - someone who is trained to save swimmers in danger.

Life jacket (life JAK-it) - a jacket that will keep you afloat in water.

Shallow (SHAL-oh) - not deep.

Supervise (SOO-pur-vize) - to watch over.

Undertow (UHN-dur-toh) - a strong current below the surface of water.

Wade (WAYD) - to walk through water.

Internet Sites

Bicycling Safety
http://www.cam.org/~skippy/sites/cycling/SafetyLinks.html
Stories, studies, statistics, and tips on everything from safe cycling practices to maintenance. Special interest sections for kids and parents, and links to many interesting sites!

Safety Tips for Kids on the Internet
http://www.fbi.gov/kids/internet/internet.htm
The FBI has set up a "safety tips for the internet" website. It has very good information about how to protect yourself online.

National School Safety Center
http://www.nssc1.org/
This site provides training and resources for preventing school crime and violence.

Home Safety
http://www.safewithin.com/homesafe/
This site helps to make the home more secure, info on the health of the home environment and other safety resources.

These sites are subject to change.

Pass It On

Educate readers around the country by passing on information you've learned about staying safe. Share your little-known facts and interesting stories. Tell others about bike riding, school experiences, and any other stuff you'd like to discuss. We want to hear from you!

To get posted on the ABDO Publishing Company website E-mail us at **"adventure@abdopub.com"**

Download a free screen saver at www.abdopub.com

Index